HOW TO BE OUR BEST SELF
IN TIMES OF CRISIS

STUART BREEN AND TOM GUNNING

HOW TO BE
Our Best Self
IN TIMES OF CRISIS

• • •

Stuart Breen and
Tom Gunning

Published 2020 by
Veritas Publications
7–8 Lower Abbey Street
Dublin 1
Ireland
publications@veritas.ie
www.veritas.ie

ISBN 978 1 84730 975 4

All photos are from The Parable Garden, Ballinesker, Wexford, www.
parablegarden.ie, unless otherwise stated: p. 12, 'Crossings'; p. 13, 'Pathways';
p. 16, 'Let your hidden self grow strong'; p. 19, 'Shell House Mandala'; p. 24,
'The Oak Pass'; p. 26, 'The Marshlands', Curracloe, Wexford; p. 29, 'A Place to
Rest'; p. 31, 'A Young Sally Tree'; p. 35, 'Entrance to the Hollow'; p. 36, 'The
Place of Masks'; p. 43, 'Young Vines'; p. 44, 'Shell House Mandala'; p. 49, 'The
Raven Point', Curracloe, Wexford; p. 52, 'Solstice Sunrise'; p. 54, 'Chrysalis';
p. 55, 'A Place to Rest'; p. 57, 'Threshold'. © Anna Thompson, 2020.

A catalogue record for this book is available from the British Library.

Designed by Padraig McCormack, Veritas Publications
Printed in the Republic of Ireland by Walsh Colour Print, Kerry

*Veritas books are printed on paper made from the wood pulp of managed
forests. For every tree felled, at least one tree is planted, thereby renewing natural
resources.*

Contents

'Be grateful for whatever comes,
because each has been sent
as a guide from beyond.'
RUMI

1

Redefining Yourself

Since the dawn of humanity we have been experiencing crises and since the dawn of humanity we have been surviving crises. From the time when we first began to traverse the ancient terrains of this planet we have been forced to seek security above all else. To be human is to be fragile, mortal. Our earliest ancestors survived in an ancient and hostile landscape fraught with threats and adversaries. These memories are stored in the most primitive parts of our brain chemistry and the desire to survive still remains our most basic instinct. The primitive brain constantly scanned the horizon for possible threats, feeling safe in the known and the familiar. We have a deep sense of unease when it comes to the unknown. It is a distrust based on an ancient fear of the unknown. When the earliest cartographers were drawing up maps of the earth many territories remained mysterious and unexplored. Where the familiar territory met the unfamiliar and unexplored the map-makers simply wrote, 'Beyond this there be dragons.'

Our desire for the familiar and that which is permanent and constant was continuously threatened by an environment that was in constant change. Our ancestors had very little understanding of the mechanics of the world. Misfortune, death, chaos and catastrophe were a constant presence and they could not be explained. So, since the dawn of history, we have been trying to find a safe place and an understanding of our volatile world through myth, story, ritual and symbol.

The greatest civilisations created a pantheon of the gods in order to try and explain the realities of fortune and misfortune. Placate the gods and times would be good, upset the gods and we expect a plague on our house. Yet the pantheon proved to be capricious and unpredictable and it was only with the advent of philosophy, mathematics and the sciences that we managed to get a rational grasp of the world around us. Despite everything, an order of sorts began to emerge, and humanity welcomed with open arms the age of reason.

As humans, we gravitate towards the familiar and the routine. It might be boring and wearisome at times but it is, at least, known and what is recognised is safe.

Understanding Change

The best type of change is that which is *chosen* and *temporary*. So, we go on holidays abroad but we still want to return to the familiar and the domestic. We pepper human experience with leisure experiences and a part of us wants the exotic and the unfamiliar when it comes to planning the family holiday: Let's do something different, it's our holidays. We also like change to be voluntary because we have control over it. We can understand it because we generated it. We can choose to change careers or even relationships and, whilst it may be challenging and difficult, we still exert a measure of control. Since the very beginning of time we have wanted to control our environment; it was safer that way.

The worst type of change is that which is *involuntary* and *permanent*. It might be difficult to end a relationship, but it is much more difficult to have a relationship ended against our will. It might be difficult to leave a profession or career for another but much worse if we are laid off permanently and unexpectedly. We lose control in these situations and we find ourselves adrift and anchorless in an ocean of uncertainty. For all sorts of reasons, the oldest parts of our brains react with stress and fear in such situations. Death has been, and remains, one of our greatest challenges. It opens a door into the complete unknown despite the best efforts at explanation from our greatest spiritual and religious traditions. Death happens to all of us and it is something we must do alone. It is permanent and we have no control over it.

We have never particularly liked it but we live in a changing world. Life is an endless process of letting go. We let go of the security of the womb and emerge into a strange world. In adolescence we let go of the innocence of childhood. Parents must let go of their children and children must let go of their parents. Between womb and tomb, life is an endless process of letting go and in all of this we have constantly to redefine ourselves. The child in us dies, the adolescent in us dies and, ultimately, we die. As much as we dislike it, life is constantly changing, and our lives are a segment of borrowed time from the cradle to the grave. A change in life that we choose is called a *life choice*; a life change that we do not choose is called a *life crisis*.

Redefining Ourselves

Life demands that we redefine ourselves and we have all done it many times. If we do not engage in that process, the teenager remains childish or the adult remains immature and refuses to commit. Life is in a constant state of flux and it refuses to stay still. We can step in the same river over and over again at the exact same spot, but the water will never be the same. The seasons change, day becomes night and birth meets death. This is our world.

We must engage with the process of redefining ourselves. This challenge hits hard when we lose a relationship or lose a job. The married person becomes single. The employed professional becomes a stay-at-home parent. The most immediate reaction is to deny that the change has taken place and as long as this denial remains, our painful feelings only worsen. The path to inner peace begins when we begin to surrender to our circumstances.

In martial arts, the best response is to move with the blow coming from the opponent, not to meet it with force. This reflex minimises any possible damage. We cannot always be in control of our circumstances, but we are always in control of our response. When the world refuses to behave the way we want it to, it is best to go with the flow and to accept it. The quicker we can achieve that response, the quicker our recovery. We cannot change anything until we accept it. If we cut ourselves, we can lament our misfortune, try to deny it and bleed out, or we can just go get it fixed.

Holding onto our old identities as professional or employed only leads to greater levels of annoyance and stress. Fighting against reality is always a losing battle where we drain our energies and diminish our resources to recreate a new identity. There is little to be gained from looking back at what is not

there anymore. If we do not have the capacity to be the thing we were, then it is best to put our energies into the thing we can be. Resistance to change tends to bring greater feelings of futility, stress and negativity. It is an immediate and instinctual reaction but to become our best selves we have to try to move on from the initial state of shock and denial.

2

Recalibrating Expectations

Denial arises as a defence against change. In Charles Dickens's masterpiece *Great Expectations*, Miss Havisham's wedding dress decays on her ageing body in her mouldering mansion. Her groom failed to turn up on her wedding day, but she refused to take off her wedding dress as she harboured some great expectation that her lover would, someday, return. She sees out her days mentally scared and emotionally imbalanced. In literature, she remains a towering symbol of denial and resistance.

When the world changes, and life changes, it is called a crisis. A crisis is not always a bad thing and it does not have to be chaotic; though, more often than not, it is. Life crises include both marriage and divorce, birth and death. A crisis is any change that affects us deeply. One way of ensuring that a crisis does not become chaotic is to accept that the world has changed and to accept that things will be different. We want things to stay the same and we want them to remain familiar, but life is not like that. The spirits of chaos feed on our denial of endings. The spirits of chaos keep us in bridal attire years after we are jilted at the altar.

LET YOUR HIDDEN SELF GROW STRONG

EPH 3:16

The Denial of Change

Archaic communities and tribes have some advantages over us when it comes to life crises. All great crisis moments are marked with special rituals called *rites of passage*. Rites of *separation* separate the whole group or individual from their previous situation or identity. Rites of *transition* help and support the individual or group to transform themselves, in order to live with a new identity. Special rites of *return* allow the individual or group to become accustomed to their new life. These rites are lavish in story, symbol, movement and ritual.

These rites ensured that transitions were marked out and clearly defined. It was clear that change or a transition had occurred, be it moving from one season to another or from childhood to adulthood. Change was never solitary. The group explained to the individual exactly what was happening to them and the group supported them through the process.

Today we are forced to face many of our life crises alone with hardly any support from the group. This would have been unthinkable to previous generations. Funeral rites and wakes remain our best example of the group supporting and helping us to interpret life crises. The group gathers around us and each stage is carefully marked out in ritual and symbol. The great advantage in all of this is that we are left in little doubt that change has occurred. Cognitively, we are being allowed to absorb and accept this change. One of the problems that arise when we encounter crises today is that we half expect the world to continue the way it was. There is no ritual to mark out the loss of a job. We mark marriage with public ceremonies and fanfare and we get divorced alone and isolated, in a lawyer's office. When the group is not there to explain what is happening and help us through, it is much harder for the reality of our new situation to seep in.

Productivity Changes

Some of our life crises are public and some are private. When we experience a public life crisis, such as a marriage or a bereavement, it is accepted that the person will be removed from ordinary productivity for a short while. Few get married today and arrive for work tomorrow. The same should apply to a bereavement. This is because crises take up a lot of our energy and resources. If a crisis is affecting us badly, the body will become very stressed and tense as an automatic reaction to something perceived to be threatening or harmful. A crisis always affects normal levels of productivity and capacity.

Archaic societies always set aside space and time for transitions or passages because they know that the change requires a lot of the person's energy, time and attention. The brain has to be given time to adjust to its new surroundings, be that a bereavement, job loss or a separation. So, quite simply, we will not be able to get as much done during a crisis as we would normally. During the Covid-19 pandemic, most productivity ceased in the country and began its return to 'normal' slowly and tentatively. This is natural and the same dynamics apply to personal crises and traumas.

Unfortunately, we are often forced to go through many of our crises alone. A relationship might break down but due to the solitary nature of the experience we are expected to behave as normal and be just as productive at work as we ordinarily were. When the group does not recognise private pain, then we have to set our own boundaries to protect ourselves. Our bodies behave differently in a crisis and they need to be given special time and space to process the many mini or major traumas.

In a crisis the brain will automatically go into fear mode because it will feel as though it is being threatened. This is called the fight or flight response. Our brains have evolved over millennia but our ancient ancestors experienced different operating systems than we do today. The oldest part of our brain, that still survives, constantly scanned the environment for threats. It performed an important function when there were serious predators around but it still gets activated any time we feel threatened.

Depending on the seriousness of the trauma or crisis we experience today, the brain might keep releasing stress hormones for days on end. Our bodies and muscles will stress and tighten due to the pressure of the stress hormone *adrenaline*. *Cortisol* is the stress hormone that is released into the brain itself to heighten its own cognitive abilities. This hormone, however, fixates the brain completely on the problem or crisis. It is trying its best to find some solution but based on a very narrow fear-based platform.

Put simply, this means that we cannot think properly during a traumatic crisis and our work and productivity levels will experience a dramatic decrease. The group of people with whom we work may not know of our crisis so we have to ensure that we take on a decreased workload. It is best to inform as many trusted people as possible that currently things

are difficult. That way we will have the time and space that we need.

We have a very intense approach to productivity in the Western world. We constantly push ourselves hard to produce and succeed. We seek promotion and greater pay as this will provide greater financial security for us and our loved ones. All of this works really well when we are happy and healthy but can become very onerous when we are experiencing the challenge of a crisis. If the world does not give us the space to work through a trauma then sometimes we have to try to create that space ourselves.

3

Rest and Recovery

A crisis can come in the form of a physical illness. This will obviously have an impact on the body and there will be physical symptoms. What is important to note, however, is that any form of a crisis, be it emotional, financial or material, will have an effect on the body. This is due to the fact that the ancient part of our brain will react to the event as if it were a threat. This part of our brain is not modern and has not yet fully caught up with our modern surroundings. That part of our brain still thinks that it is battling predators in Palaeolithic forests.

When a person is faced with a crisis, the most immediate changes that they will experience will be to their body. They will feel increased stress and tension in their body. They will find it difficult to sleep and they will experience a loss of appetite. It is as if parts of the regular systems of our bodies have shut down and this is exactly what has happened. If the ancient brain interprets our crisis as akin to the predator in the forest thousands of years ago, it reacts accordingly. As far as the brain is concerned, what we need to do is think fast, run fast or fight.

The brain, therefore, has to make some pretty quick decisions in terms of where resources are going to go.

Adrenaline will ready the muscles for fight or flight. Cortisol will focus the brain on immediate problem-solving. There is, therefore, little time to think about eating or digesting food. The brain takes resources from these bodily systems to fight the threat. If we are threatened in the forest by a predator that could eat us, it is hardly a good idea to have a nap and switch off our alert system. As far as the brain is concerned, in a time of crisis we need to stay alert so sleep will definitely be disrupted. This is rather unfortunate because in a crisis we really need to be able to switch off, but instead we face endless nights awake ruminating on the problem.

Oftentimes a crisis will last for a long time, so we allow the primitive brain to constantly trigger these effects in our bodies. The brain just wants to survive and can actually act in a rather selfish manner. We might be extremely tired and losing weight but our ancient brain will be deciding that this does not really matter as long as we can stay alive. So, during a time of crisis, we have to be aware of what is going on in our bodies and that a very obsolete and not-fit-for-purpose piece of brain software is running the show. The body has no choice but to react to the flood of stress chemicals released by the brain.

Nurturing the Body

The human body will take a huge hit during a time of crisis. Our thoughts and emotions are real physical things that are housed in different parts of our bodies. Think back to a time when things were really good, like a nice sunny foreign holiday. Remember how good our body felt. It was responding to the relaxing and happy chemicals that were being constantly washed through our body. In a crisis, our body has to deal with a nervous system that is under constant pressure from the chemicals released from the brain through the sympathetic nervous system. We have to process a lot of emotional material, which is also exhausting on the body. We will be using up vast quantities of reserves and this is something that needs to be addressed. The key point here is that we cannot trust the old, obsolete software to handle this crisis properly; therefore, the more advanced parts of our brain need to be listened to as we begin to try to come to terms with our new reality.

Rest and Recovery

A crisis is a change and, in many instances, this change will be permanent. The positive thing to keep in mind during a crisis is that it has an inherent process. Whilst the primitive brain can cause us all sorts of problems during the initial stages of a crisis, we also have a bank of resources both in ourselves and in the support of others that will help us to complete the change. Remember how the ancients dealt with a crisis: they mapped out the three stages – separation, transition and return – that were involved to get themselves through the crisis. The first was a complete acknowledgment through ritual, story and symbol that change had occurred. These are the rites of separation.

What increases the levels of trauma to the body is our refusal to accept that the change has occurred, possibly irrevocably. Once we accept that the change has happened, despite the pain of that acknowledgement, it is only then that we can proceed on to the process of returning to our best selves. Once we can begin to accept the new reality in which we find ourselves, the body will begin to relax.

Remember how the martial artist went with the flow of the attack and did not try to resist. We need to allow the body to run off the effects of the stress hormones. When this happens, it can begin to rest and recover. We can then move forward from resistance to embracing the transformational process. We need to give our body the time it needs to run off the effects of stress and restore the energies that have been used up during the crisis. All of this is important so that what began as a financial or emotional crisis does not become a physical one as well.

Natural Balance

We live with a particular mindset when it comes to productivity. It is a Western consumerist model based on the fact that the more money we earn the more we can buy. In the Western model people like to make profit and towards that end there can be a constant push from our bosses, supervisors and even our teachers to produce the best results. This is also a model that is leading to very high rates of depression, stress and burnout. It is a model that is very threatening to our well-being and out of touch with the natural rhythms of productivity and rest.

The earth is the most productive entity that exists. It produces all the resources and food that we need to survive. It is helpful to observe its natural rhythms of productivity. The earth is governed by annual crises called seasons. If an observer from another planet arrived during autumn, that individual would be of the view that the planet was in the midst of a huge catastrophe. Everything would be decaying, atrophying and dying. The fields would look scarce and scant, covered with a carpet of deadening stalks and mildewed foliage. The trees would appear to be dying whilst shedding a decaying cloak of leaves to the ground.

Yet in the natural rhythms of the earth, death is part of life. Death is the opposite of birth but it is not the opposite of life. In the natural rhythm of things, death and crises are fundamental to new life and growth. What we know is that the earth in autumn is merely entering a great period of rest after its bountiful harvest. The earth cannot be in a perpetual state of growth and harvest; no living system operates that way. The only way that the earth can be productive is if it can lie fallow during autumn and winter to enjoy its period of rest and recovery. It is only based on this principle that the earth can be productive. To compare and contrast the earth's natural approach to productivity and harvest to the Western model adopted by the office block and high street is interesting, to say the least.

The earth must recover after its period of intense activity during spring and summer, yet the ancients' understanding was that the earth was a mirror of our own systems. After all, both are living systems. When we meet a crisis in our lives, our bodies and systems are forced into a heightened state of activity as we try to absorb and deal with the emotional and mental fallout of the experience; therefore, in order for us to recover and be our best selves during a crisis, we too have to enter a period of rest, but this affects productivity and projects.

Shame and Guilt

Two unwelcome guests during a crisis are shame and guilt. Sometimes humans get it wrong and the crisis feels as if it is self-inflicted. Shame is one of the lowest energetic vibrations the body has to deal with. Sometimes these feelings can even visit us if the crisis is not of our making.

A crisis like Covid-19 can present us with a lot of time on our hands but if that is coupled with the loss of a job or a business, we might be tempted into thinking that we still need to keep being productive. It is very difficult for us to break the cycle of productivity as sometimes we actually become addicted to the presence of the stress hormones in our bodies flooding us with waves of excited energy.

It is vital, however, just like the earth, to rest after a crisis and let the body repair. It means that we should not try to take on big projects around the home or garden. This is to completely misunderstand what our body needs. It has just run the gauntlet of a marathon of stressful events and it cannot be asked to do any more. Remember, a crisis always affects our bodies and if we do not attend to the stresses and strains on our physical systems then a physical illness could easily accompany our crisis.

In the Western production paradigm, we should always be producing and we should always be able to show that we are active. Even a lot of our leisure time has been taken up with physical exercise and exertion as opposed to physical rest and leisure. It would appear that our *work* is oftentimes our *worth*. If we decide during a crisis to be responsible to our body and minimise the amount we need to do, this is not laziness; it is being smart. If we allow our mind to dredge up feelings of laziness when in fact our body needs to rest, this will, in effect, only stress our body even further and perpetuate the cycle of the release of stress hormones into our system.

The Hidden Wonders of Rest

Try taking a leisurely stroll some evening and observe the number of runners, cyclists and brisk walkers who pass you out. Life, it would appear, is a race and slowing down is anathema to the modern lifestyle. Imagine trying to explain all of that to a tree in winter: you're not concentrating; you're getting left behind; your work rate is totally unacceptable; you're too slow! Nature knows the wisdom of rest and we would do well to learn from her rhythms.

The ground rests because the earth has to produce a good harvest. Properly understood, productivity comes after rest.

As we mentioned earlier, there are three phases to a crisis: separation, transition and return. Returning to a new and changed life after a crisis will be one of the most productive things that we will ever do, which is why it is important to mirror the dynamics of the natural world. Nature knows what it is doing and it contains a perennial wisdom observed by all our ancient forebears.

After a crisis we will be different and the world might also be very different and the rest period gives our mind and our body the time and space that it needs to change. At a certain stage in a caterpillar's life it is attacked from within by special cells called imaginal cells. The caterpillar tries to fight back but is overcome. It then builds itself a cocoon to die in but death is not necessarily the opposite of new life. During cocooning the metamorphosis begins and soon the fabric rips open and a beautiful butterfly emerges. The caterpillar experienced a huge crisis, rested in its cocoon and then returned to the world transformed, resplendent and able to fly. The caterpillar mirrors the dynamics of a crisis when 'separation, transition and return' become 'walk, cocoon and fly'.

During sleep, our mind and body are actually very active repairing, learning, organising and regulating. We do not see this but it is happening. During prolonged periods of rest over weeks or even months our minds and bodies also become active in ways that might not be observable to us. Our body, during a restful crisis, may be getting its first real rest for twenty years. Repairs, long overdue, might be given time to heal worn systems, energies and brain circuitry.

During the transitionary phase of a crisis, the body and mind have to readjust, rebuild and redefine. Rest is central to this process. We do not have to know what goes on in sleep to reap the wonderful health benefits and the same applies to a period of resting up from normal activity. The stressed brain will only think in a very fixated and narrow way during the initial stages of a crisis while we can be experiencing some degree of shock or trauma. This type of thinking will not help a more in-depth process of redefining oneself and recognising new opportunities and ways to be in the world post-crisis.

Redefining one's identity is a very creative process and, therefore, the brain must engage in creative thinking. Creative thinking, however, is a very slow process as many options must be tried and tested before we can re-emerge from our cocoon back into the world. In order to be creative, the brain needs rest, new stimuli and as much immersion in nature as possible. Creative thinking does not always occur at the conscious level, which means that the brain can be trying new ideas, relationships and possibilities without us being aware of it. Nobody sits down at a desk and decides to have a eureka moment. These moments just happen once the subconscious mind has been given the time and space to carry out its own operations unhindered.

Our entire human ancestry and survival is based on the brain's ability to think fast during an initial trauma and then to think slow during the redefining process. The ancients created ritual times and spaces to contain the transitionary processes of redefining the self. What remains wonderful and encouraging for anyone going through a crisis is that the mind and body contain thousands of years of built-up intelligence and wisdom. Becoming our best selves during a crisis sometimes means getting out of

our own way. It means surrendering to and trusting the hidden wonders of our ancient mind and body to heal itself.

5

Expanding Consciousness

Our conscious mind is that part of our mental world that is aware of particular things at any given moment. Whatever we are thinking about or listening to or trying to absorb makes up the activity of the conscious mind. Our conscious mind is only able to hold so many thoughts at any given moment. Some people can multitask and hold more thoughts and activities in their conscious mind. Due to the greater presence of social media and endless news outlets in our lives, we are bombarded with billions of bytes of information per second. The mind simply cannot process all of this information and, in fact, it is estimated that we process only about 2 per cent of the information that is coming at us at any given time. So, the interesting part of that sum is that we are missing out on about 98 per cent of the reality around us in any given moment; therefore, there is a lot going on around us that we are not paying attention to. Inside that 98 per cent might be a lot of good ideas about how to be our best self during a crisis.

Our minds tend to mull over past events and they definitely worry and ruminate over possible future events, so we often find it difficult to be really present in any given moment.

Mindfulness is a practice that tries to get us to be more present to the *now* of our lives. Now is the only thing that is actually happening. The past is gone, and the future might never actually happen. During a crisis phase in our lives we need to look for possibilities and opportunities that will allow us to exist in the world in a different way. We need to pay attention to new job opportunities or new relationship networks. All of these prospects or potentialities can only be found in the present moment, in the conversations we are listening to and the information we are absorbing.

The nature of the universe and the world is that it is in a constant state of flux and change. New possibilities and opportunities are coming into existence all of the time so it is important to open the filters of our mind to the present moment and really try to absorb what is going on around us. This can be very challenging during a painful crisis. The instinct might be to withdraw from the world to protect ourselves but this is not how we become our best self during a crisis. We become our best self by actually engaging with the world even more and expanding our notion of who we are and the supports that are actually available to us.

Expeditions and Mountaintops

There is something about mountaintops and crises. Throughout human history the great enlightened ones found their enlightenment on top of mountains. Their lives were undeniably a bit unclear before this event, but they always went on expeditions to the mountains to seek new and greater

insights into themselves and the world around them. Moses and Jacob, Jesus and Mohammad and the ancient Rishis of India all made their way to the mountaintop for greater clarity about things during times of confusion. They went there to expand their consciousness and it is not too difficult to see why.

When the stressed brain is initially trying to cope with a crisis it becomes fixated on that particular problem. It thinks only about the lost loved one or the lost job. It laments, mourns and thinks of ways to retrieve what is gone. It battles the now and demands that the world give back that which the world cannot give back. The rested brain, washed with the calmer parasympathetic nervous system, begins to see the bigger picture of what life is about. Imagine yourself on the street of a small village looking up towards the nearest mountain. It is

inviting you to climb it. It beckons you to leave the small world of the village and the tiny world of your fixated pain and loss.

As you begin to climb, you feel yourself going upwards and upwards. Every so often you sit down to rest and take in the view. You keep going upwards and again you sit down to take in the view. What is happening to your world each time you sit down to rest? It is expanding and getting bigger. As you ascend the mountain, the horizon all around you expands and expands and you begin to see more. You see the entire village and the next town, and in the distance you see the outskirts of a great city. You see rivers, lakes and an entire network of roads. Your world has just gotten much, much bigger.

Ascending the mountain is like opening the filters of our mind into the now and the present moment. This process does not fight the moment; in fact, it does the opposite. It begins to explore the now as it surrenders to what is actually happening instead of what it wants to happen. During the Covid-19 lockdown, people suddenly became stay-at-home mums or dads. They became homeschoolers. Within that reality there were so many new opportunities. They could become really involved in the lives of their children, freed from the stress of work and the endless trips to clubs, piano lessons, etc. As well as the challenges the lockdown presented, so too there were many really positive opportunities. Relationships could deepen and tired and worn bodies could rest and recuperate.

Roles and Relationships

When the conscious mind becomes less active, still and attentive to the moment, the subconscious mind has a greater opportunity to present possibilities and opportunities.

We had a business but now we are stay-at-home parents. We used to be really busy and stressed but now we can relax. We used to be in a relationship with one person but now we have endless possibilities to be in other relationships or just single. Sometimes the roles we have are like masks we wear. Removing one mask, if even for a while, can bring a sense of liberation.

A crisis always brings freedom from something. We might rail and fight against it, because the primitive brain does not like change and is threatened by insecurity, and transition and transformation are never familiar to us. We are becoming something new and that can be frightening, or it can free us to explore new relationships and roles.

We can imagine ourselves sitting on top of the mountain of our own lives. We can embrace a spirit of curiosity and become explorers of the possibilities presented in this panoramic view. We can go on an expedition into our own abilities and capabilities and look at the vast range of relationships in our lives. We have personal relationships, both familial and with friends. We have interpersonal relationships with our town, neighbourhood, clubs and organisations. The world is offering itself to our imagination and creativity. Let us live each moment deliberately by exploring and accepting all new relationships and realities.

Nourishment

The architects of some of the greatest megalithic sites on the planet believed that the cosmos was in a constant state of crisis. Denied a scientific world view, they were left with mythological narratives to understand the world around them. The ancient moon-watchers observed an orb that was full in the sky but then waned into nothingness. This was a crisis if ever there was one. The moon had literally just disappeared!

The builders of Newgrange observed the sun slowly descend into the horizon every winter solstice. They had no scientific knowledge of how it would return or if it would return. So, they built a mound to capture the final embers of a dying sun. The moon would disappear but could somehow regenerate itself. The fading sunlight of the winter solstice could somehow be completely replenished by the time of the dawn of the summer solstice. Though mysterious to the prescientific mindset, there seemed to be a principle of regeneration operating in the universe.

All of life, both human and planetary, experiences crises but after death, atrophy and decay come rejuvenation, renewal and regeneration. It is simply a process and dynamic that is woven into the fabric of all life including human life. Nothing stays the same, everything changes. It is important, therefore, that we turn our attention to readying ourselves for the return to full life after the crisis. It is important that we nourish all the different systems that we rely on in anticipation of the return of our own inner moon and our own inner sun. It is an encouraging and important truth to note that after death comes life, after decay comes rebirth and after crisis comes a return.

One particular example of a crisis is burnout. The mind is very powerful and it can propel us into a level of activity that the body simply cannot keep up with. The mind, for a while, can override the warning systems that the body sends, and it can push the physical systems way beyond their ability. Eventually, however, when we reach the threshold of irretrievable damage, the body switches everything down. The primitive part of the brain then kicks in and overrides the mind and turns off the switch in our internal power stations. We have reached a burnout and, like any house that is burnt out, there is only the visible structure remaining.

Body Needs

If our physical home is destroyed, we can rebuild it based on the original footprint. It will not be the same but it can be restored. We can also rebuild ourselves after a burnout but it takes a lot of time and it begins with nourishing the physical body. Whether it is a burnout or a crisis of another kind, the primitive brain will always perceive it as an attack on its physical survival. A deluge of stress hormones is released. In order to move through the process of convincing the brain to close the floodgates of liquid stress, we have to slowly but surely convince it that it will not be threatened again. The stressed brain after a crisis remains on high alert for quite some time so it is important to slowly begin to reassure it that we are now taking care of our body. The body will pick up all these comforting signals and send them back to the brain.

Nourishing the body is key to returning ourselves to the world ready to start again. The body will more than likely be filled with stresses and strains after the initial crisis. Muscles will be tense and tightened and there could be any number of toxins in the body. The functioning of organs might need to be regulated and blood sugars returned to normal. We will need our body to be in good shape when we return to a new 'normal'.

During the Covid-19 pandemic people had time to nourish themselves properly. One of the first things that deteriorates during busyness and stress is our diet and this is a contributing factor to burnout on many different levels. Quite simply, it takes time to cook good food and that is why food that is bad for us is called 'fast food'. During a crisis it is possible that our immune system has also taken a hit. We might be more prone to colds and infections. This is because our immune system does not function properly during periods of stress. One of the best ways to nourish our immune system is by eating plenty of fresh fruit and vegetables along with wholegrain foods. It takes more time to source, prepare and cook fresh food but quite often time is the one thing that a crisis gives us. We need to use it to nourish and repair our own bodies. It takes around thirty days to form a new habit so we need to try to maintain our new way of cooking and eating over as long a period as we can.

We can also take this time to nourish our body in other ways. Relaxing baths help to relay to the primitive brain that things are changing, and we are moving through our crisis. We have to constantly reassure the body that we are taking care of it because if we are not taking care of it, this is perceived as a threat and leads to stress. The modern paradigm of productivity and activity suits machines and robots but it does not suit humans.

Learning

We can also nourish ourselves mentally. We can read the books we have always wanted to read or take an online course in something that really interests us. It is very important to nourish the mind with something new. In a crisis something is gone and part of the recovery is to accept that it is gone. If our crisis was brought on by pressures in the banking or financial sector then it is important not to spend this time learning more about finance. We do not need to keep feeding the thing that damaged us in the first place as this does not help us to redefine and recreate ourselves.

The moon inside us that will return will be called the new moon. It is not called the return of the old moon. It is good to stimulate ourselves with new mental content to promote the growth of new neurological networks in our brains. We can allow our brains this time to expand and scan the boundaries of our old lives for new openings and new pathways to explore.

Despite our experiences at school, we can rekindle inside ourselves a curiosity and desire to learn new things. There is a huge difference between the rote learning that we did at school and genuine learning based on interest and personal development.

Learning is one of our most fundamental abilities, yet it is also one that we often dismiss as irrelevant outside of a school context. Learning new skills and abilities is a key to unlocking and opening all those doors that slammed shut so abruptly during our crisis. We can invest in ourselves by learning new insights and gaining new perspectives on the world. The

renewal of our ability to learn how to become a new person in our new world is one of the keystones of becoming our best self during a crisis. Our ability to learn is on a par with our ability to breathe. To say we do not know how to learn is like saying we do not know how to breathe.

Relish Our Experiences

It is difficult to rid ourselves of the shackles of the productivity paradigm and there is a certain shame and guilt that comes from judging ourselves as no longer contributing to society. We measure success based on financial gain through professional endeavour as opposed to voluntary or charitable activity. There is an incessant 'push forward' mindset ingrained in Western society that fails to appreciate the necessity of periodically investing in ourselves as a people. Our activities and use of time might very well change during a crisis but our experiences of rest, nourishment, learning and recovery are a really important investment in ourselves as balanced human beings.

Doing nothing is important. We need energy to return to the world after our crisis and energy is expended through activity. The way we replenish our energy and vitality for life is by basking in blissful nothingness as all our systems are repaired. Growing our own food or spending time with important people in our lives may not be productive in the strict sense but it is vital to replenish and regenerate ourselves. Time stretches to both ends of eternity but the opportunities and experiences that present themselves in any given moment should be seized because we can waste them. Work and relationships usually return in some form so while we are experiencing a hiatus in the betwixt-and-between time, we can relish what comes our way.

7

The Complete Self

During a crisis it is always tempting to look back and remember when times were better. This can be painful, especially if those experiences are never coming back. When we did feel good it was not something that simply happened in our thoughts. Thoughts are very fine streams of energy but do not in themselves have feeling, yet they can impact on our emotional self. Our physical body can feel pain and discomfort or a lack of these things, but our organs do not specifically feel loss or hope or belonging. If we want to feel good again we need to connect with many different layers in the strata of our own being.

There are many different layers to us, and we need to replenish these and nourish these to ready ourselves for our return to the new normal. There are different energy systems that can be affected during the trauma of a crisis and there is a spiritual self that can be weakened or truncated. There is nothing quite as bad as an amputated human spirit. These fine energies inside us can be difficult to identify but we will feel it when they too are damaged. It is not within the brief of this short book to explore the landscape of what makes us up, but we have touched on some already and within this chapter we will address some more.

We spoke about the need of nourishing the physical self through good food, exercise and general self-care. Stimulating our mental processes through learning and enquiring about the world around us can rebuild mental confidence. We will be able to assess our physical requirements by our own level of energy in any given day. Remember, we will not be able to be as productive as we once were so things will have to slow down. We will feel the level of stress hormones in our body through feelings of tension, irritability and an inability to sleep. Learn to avoid the triggers that set off the stress response.

The Emotional Self

If we have been through a Western educational system, we will have used and developed many cerebral capabilities as we tried to learn and understand a variety of subjects. Sometimes the emotional self gets left behind and success as a human being is assessed on our ability to simply retain information. We can get a great feeling of satisfaction in succeeding in this system. Yet all the while different parts of our emotional self can be ignored or devalued. It is important to stress that the emotional self should not be equated with the usual term 'emotional', as in 'he or she was very emotional'. This can be sometimes perceived as being a moment of weakness and losing control of ourselves. In fact, the emotional self is much deeper and far more subtle than this commonplace meaning.

There are important emotions that constantly need to be nourished and protected. It is important to love and to feel that we are loved. This can be a painful area to examine for many but love does not have to be confined to romantic attachments or familial bonds. These can be broken and form the basis of a crisis in the first place. Yet loving feelings can also be displayed and nourished throughout a wide network of connections with others in a variety of ways. A broken heart might take years to fix but, in the meantime, it can be supported by ancillary feelings like belonging and being appreciated. It is a fundamental human need to feel that we belong to a group and love itself is simply a very strong and deep-rooted feeling of belonging. So, take note of how we feel emotionally as we journey through the difficult terrain of a crisis.

Before our crisis we might have felt valued in a job or relationship that was then taken from us. This may have been a

source of meaning. We felt good because we felt needed and we fulfilled an important role. That is still an important feeling to have, that we have a place in this world and that we are needed. We can fulfil this emotional need by simply getting involved in life again and especially around acts of kindness and service. If we wake up any morning with an agenda to help others, we have a busy day ahead of us. Needless to say, we might not do this but it is important to know that the world needs us despite our own possible beliefs to the contrary.

Verbalise Our Needs

It is important to try to connect as much as we can with others during a crisis. Since our earliest times on this planet we have evolved as very social creatures and when these bonds weaken, we are affected. Often, we can live in very populated urban areas and still feel very isolated. During the Covid-19 crisis people experienced lockdown and cocooning for the first time in living memory. It is important, however, to remember that there are a variety of ways to stay connected and nourish any possible feelings of isolation and meaninglessness. We need to draw up a list of people who are important to us and then reach out over a variety of social media platforms or simple phone calls or letter writing. To serve the Western productivity paradigm, a lot of us moved to the city and other populous centres. The irony of this urban evolution after the industrial era was that for many of us it meant that we have never felt so alone. To be human is to be social so it is important to monitor that particular need when we are going through a challenging time.

Words create worlds, and in a crisis they become particularly useful. In the Hebrew creation myth our world was created with words. Before the Divinity spoke there was chaos and the earth was only a 'formless void'. The Divinity then spoke and everything came into being. Then the Divinity rested. We have been creating our world with our words all our life. Have we ever said any of the following? 'Will you marry me?' 'I'd like to study that.' 'I'd like to live there.' 'I think I'll apply for that job.' As we will see, our words create massive changes in our lives, so they play a very significant role during a crisis. A crisis can feel good or bad and our words are a wonderful navigational tool as we wander through this time.

Before a crisis our lives can become quite stagnant and governed by routine. We like it like that because it is familiar and very predictable, but we cannot do much with our lives caught up in a comfortable routine. It lacks creativity, change and transformation. The universe, however, favours change, be it seasonal or the phases of the planetary orbits. Sometimes people will create a crisis to get movement or flow into their lives by ending a job or relationship. Sometimes life will just do it for us. We can sit back and let life happen or we can become a creator of our own world with our words. Words are like pebbles being thrown into a pond; each pebble creates a ripple that moves outward into the world. Our words are the same, they ripple out into the very fabric of the universe and begin to attract what it is we want, slowly, subtly and over time.

There is a great power in asking. We need to let people know what we want. When we are weak there will be many people who are strong around us. It is okay to rely on them. It is okay to ask for help because it is all cyclical and we will someday help them. When we are in a crisis, nothing has gone wrong; we are just experiencing the world and the way it operates. There is always a letting go and a freedom in a crisis. It may not feel good because change is challenging but we can redefine and create a new identity and a new world.

Ask for help. Ask for advice. Seek out information and let the world know what you want. The Divinity spoke and there was light. Speak out and ask for your share of prosperity and good fortune from the world. Use your words to dispel the shadows of despair and confusion. You have lost much, you have let go and you have shed your cloak of familiarity but you are still very, very much alive.

Create

The most difficult crises are the ones that we feel we have brought upon ourselves and others. We do not like it when we fall short of the mark of what it is to be human. We are, unfortunately, bombarded with ideas of perfection continuously. The most obvious one is body image and shape and the result is body shaming. Social media tends to present the best of people's lives, not the worst. We display our best side in front of others. Yet it all leads to a skewed version of what it is to be human. Human is marvellous, but it is also a mess and anyone who has lived it for a few years knows this to be true. The point is that that is true for everyone, not just you.

Everyone struggles with the human condition and it is not perfect. There is an old Jewish term, *yetzer hara*. It refers to that dimension in all humans to get things wrong. It identifies it and allows all human beings to participate in that human trait. We get things wrong and we can get things wrong quite often. We know what pain is like and we do not like the feeling of pain. We want to avoid it and there can be a lot of pain in a crisis. Another term that comes from the Hebrew tradition is *felix culpa*. A translation of the Latin might be 'happy fault'. It refers

to the fall and the fault within Adam and Eve, which in turn brought about redemption. *Felix culpa* sees the fortunate aspects of unfortunate events. Nothing is completely good or bad within itself; there are always elements of both. It would be so much easier if being human was straightforward but it is not and it is important to realise that that applies to all humans despite public displays of perfection.

It is important to allow an element of compassion to rise up inside of ourselves towards all of our actions that have fallen short of the mark. Allow the corresponding amount of compassion to be shown to others for the times when they have also messed things up. The incredibly wonderful aspect of being human is that this messiness is fertile ground for growth and change. Think of what we have to do to fields to make them fertile. We plough, harrow and repeatedly break open the soil and then we fill it with manure.

Yet this is how growth, change, creativity and transformation take place. The same applies to us. The best of being human can emerge from the worst of being human. The miraculous human realties of healing and forgiveness all take place in the shadow of brokenness and heartbreak. So, it does not matter how our crisis arrived, it is still the fertile place for change and growth.

Flow and Movement

Like Miss Havisham, we can choose to stay in a crisis forever but that requires effort. The universe is constantly changing, and our period of crisis will change too. Yes, another crisis might come along but it is not an infernal type of cycle. It is more a spiral and we grow stronger and wiser with each one that comes our way. So, the way that we find our route out of the crisis is by mirroring the way nature works and that is by bringing flow, change and movement into our lives. Water stagnates if it does not move and we stagnate if we do not involve ourselves in the world. The safest thing to do in a crisis is to lock ourselves in a room, secluded from the world. It is true that maybe another crisis might not find us but it is hardly living. It is also to deny the fact that the final and third stage of a crisis is 'return'.

Energy flows with movement and during a crisis it is important to be active and move our body. Movement burns off stress hormones but it also creates activity. Movement is like throwing those pebbles into the pond and sending out ripples and waves of energy. It is important to create new experiences for ourselves and seek out the people and things that will help us out of our crisis. We need to get in the car and drive places. We need to walk down streets and look at notices to fill our minds with fresh new ideas about what is possible in our lives right now. Life does not happen to us; we create our lives, we create our world. There is a responsibility in that fact but there is also energy, excitement and freedom.

Journaling

During the transitionary phase of a crisis, old ways of seeing and doing things will be slipping away and new ways of being in the world will be emerging. In a crisis there is always the mourning of the old, along with the realisation of the new. It is important to put some sort of structure on this new thing that is emerging into our conscious mind. We will be receiving new ideas and insights but these can easily be lost in everyday distractions if they are not written down and noted. This is why journaling is such a helpful activity during a change.

Journaling does not necessarily have to be a log of emotional upheaval. It can involve identifying emotions and

trying to contain them in some structure, be that the written word or drawings but it can also just be a way of helping us to redefine ourselves. We have to do some of the work to emerge from our cocoon of transition but the universe and our own subconscious mind does a lot of the work too. Through effort, movement and activity we are sending out messages to the universe. Like ripples in the pond, those energetic thoughts, intentions and emotions will begin to change the fabric of reality. Doorways will open and new thresholds of opportunity will be revealed where we saw only brick walls and dead ends. Reality is not fixed, it is fluid.

The subconscious mind works much faster and more efficiently than the conscious mind and during the fertile time of a crisis it will send visions, images, insights and breakthroughs that we need to capture when they emerge. An insight or eureka moment can manifest itself at any moment but it can drift away in a sea of distractions. When we journal, we become the cartographer of our own world and there is an immense power in physically writing material down with a pen or pencil. Our journal can also be filled with drawings, paintings, verse or just simple ramblings. It can be our own private repository of hopes and dreams, a birthing place of the new self but also the testing ground for new ideas.

Failure is an essential tool as we begin to redefine and create our best self. Some ideas will have to be killed off as they can gain no traction in the rough practicalities of the real world. Our journal can be the crucible of this sometimes very difficult process of testing and failing. An idea for a new business or job might emerge from the subconscious mind replete with a fabulous energy but it just won't work in the real world. Killing off attractive and fanciful ideas is a very necessary part of the process of creating the new thing but it can be unpleasant. 'Fail fast and fail often' is the motto of many big enterprises and creative industries because it is how we create. Our journal can be the factory floor where the new self is assembled amidst the bits and pieces of failed dreams and practical possibilities.

The Return

Time slows down during a crisis as we experience a suspension of normal activities. A crisis is not something that we need to survive or get over. Instead it is something we need to embrace in order to become our best selves. We have mapped and noted the different expressions of what a crisis looks like in nature, the cosmos and the rites and rituals of archaic societies. A crisis is a process of growth and transmutation where the spirit of life roams freely in the land of death, planting new seeds for a new harvest.

During the Covid-19 pandemic many people found themselves in a strange and unfamiliar landscape. Jobs and businesses were shut and people found themselves forced into long periods of reflection about how they lived their lives. New insights and perspectives were gained about the 'old normal' before the pandemic. Fatality and tragedy led to mourning, but people also mourned their old familiar lifestyles. Yet a crisis will always bring growth and fresh new insight about our lives if it is grasped and handled properly.

People decided they could work from home, which would be kinder to the planet and allow the forging of better relationships at home with children. People realised they did not need to spend quite as much money as they had been spending. The 'old normal' included a lot of waste born out of excessive lifestyles and a myopic view of how we can live. A crisis can always be the fertile ground for new insights and new perspectives.

To become our best selves in a crisis we first accept that it is happening, and we surrender to the process of redefining ourselves and our relationships with the world and with others. We learn to slow down and rest and in that fallow land of reflection we begin to see things differently as we dream new dreams and cultivate new ideas in the crucible of our imagination. A crisis can be painful but remember, nothing is only good or bad. The ancients recognised that there was always some boon or gift to be received no matter what the nature of the crisis. We are here to learn, grow and mature and sometimes the veils of the ordinary world have to be lifted for us to enter or embrace that process. We will always choose to stay with the familiar, to live comfortably in the centre of things but life demands that we periodically journey to thresholds at the far edges and borderlands of our existence to expand our limited consciousness.

The cosmos and universe are in a state of constant flux and we simply cannot keep hold of the secure and the familiar for long periods of our existence here. We might prefer the comfort of inertia but that only leads to decay and stagnation. We might have been shattered and shaken to the core of our existence but that is exactly what the rumblings of death and rebirth look like in our lives. We need to let go of the old and embrace the new life that is waiting.

A Birthing

Some new thing has been born in the womb of our existence and we will have to navigate some different way of relating to a new world. The return to the world needs to be handled in the exact same manner as we would handle any birthing process; therefore, the expectations that we have of ourselves in this new reality need to be tapered to reflect the abilities and capabilities of the newborn. Yet again we will have to take a stand against the incessant demands of the Western paradigm of achievement and production. We expect very little from the newborn and we let them play all day long and we go to great lengths to protect the sapling tree or sprouting harvest.

In the same way, we need to be gentle on ourselves and be compassionate with the pace of things in this new landscape of our best self. Things will be slow at first and we have to get used to things being different. A plane needs a long runway to take off and its ascent is gradual so think aviation and not rocket science as we reach for our new destination. It takes a lot more energy out of us to deal with the unfamiliar instead of the familiar and the world will have changed after a crisis. Take the guilt out of an easier pace and more conscious engagement with the everyday things. The world after the arrival of Covid-19 is slower, careful and more thoughtful and this is what the world feels like at the end of any crisis. It is important to set realistic targets for what is possible instead of what is probable.

We can listen to the message that the ancients have left for us in ritual and myth that everything is in a state of flux and our crisis will come to an end. We can also surrender some control to the universe and trust that good things are coming our way if we honestly and with integrity attempt to be our best selves. Have the courage and belief that we can push at the edges of what appears to be the real world and feel for the soft spots in the hard wall of reality. The world is not fixed and it offers its own unfolding story to our imagination.

When we reach the edges of our own familiar world and we begin to step beyond the boundaries of the known, we are beginning the necessary process of expanding our consciousness. As our world gets bigger, the parameters of our crisis get smaller and smaller and the pain and discomfort will shrink as we build up a network of new experiences and new relationships. Let us make our own journey to our own mountaintop. We can watch the horizon of our life expand and as we do so we can embrace the panorama of the redefined self. As we become our best selves, let the time of mourning wither with the autumn leaves as this new identity breaks ground with the green shoots of hope.